HAL•LEONARD®
VIOLIN PLAY-ALONG

AUDIO ACCESS INCLUDED

Gypsy Jazz

VOL. 80

PLAYBACK+
Speed • Pitch • Balance • Loop

To access audio visit:
www.halleonard.com/mylibrary

Enter Code
6244-2548-5276-0551

ISBN 978-1-5400-5235-3

Jon Vriesacker, violin
Audio arrangements by Peter Deneff
Recorded and Produced by Jake Johnson
at Paradyme Productions

HAL•LEONARD®

Visit Hal Leonard Online at
www.halleonard.com

Contact us:
Hal Leonard
7777 West Bluemound Road
Milwaukee, WI 53213
Email: info@halleonard.com

In Europe, contact:
Hal Leonard Europe Limited
42 Wigmore Street
Marylebone, London, W1U 2RN
Email: info@halleonardeurope.com

In Australia, contact:
Hal Leonard Australia Pty. Ltd.
4 Lentara Court
Cheltenham, Victoria, 3192 Australia
Email: info@halleonard.com.au

After You've Gone

Words by Henry Creamer
Music by Turner Layton

All of Me

Words and Music by Seymour Simons and Gerald Marks

Coquette

Words by Gus Kahn
Music by Carmen Lambardo and John Green

Daphne

By Django Reinhardt

Dark Eyes

Russian Cabaret Song

I Got Rhythm

Music and Lyrics by George Gershwin and Ira Gershwin

Time After Time

from the Metro-Goldwyn-Mayer Picture IT HAPPENED IN BROOKLYN

Words by Sammy Cahn
Music by Jule Styne

D.S. al Coda

CODA

Swing 42

By Django Reinhardt